The Heart of
the Matter

D1560270

G-5582

The Heart of the Matter

Church Music as Praise, Prayer, Proclamation, Story, and Gift

Paul Westermeyer

GIA Publications, Inc.
Chicago

G-5582
© Copyright 2001
GIA Publications, Inc.
7404 S. Mason Ave., Chicago, IL 60638
www.giamusic.com

ISBN: 1-57999-151-3
Printed in U.S.A.

To
Sally
and our children,
Chris, Tim, Rachel, and Rebecca,
who taught me how to sing

Table of Contents

Preamble 9

Chapter 1: Church Music as Praise 11

Chapter 2: Church Music as Prayer .21

Chapter 3: Church Music as Proclamation 31

Chapter 4: Church Music as Story 39

Chapter 5: Church Music as Gift of God 47

Preamble

This little booklet[1] began as lectures for the Sewanee Church Music Conference at Monteagle, Tennessee, from July 17–23, 2000. When Keith Shafer asked me to give the lectures, he allowed me considerable latitude in the choice of subject matter, but he suggested that the contents of my book *The Church Musician*[2] would be most relevant to the Conference. Since I was to give five lectures, and since there are five points in the chapter on "The Heart of the Matter," which I have wanted for some time to expand, I decided to use that chapter as the basis for these lectures.

To discipline myself with a Biblical grounding without choosing texts that would automatically confirm my biases, somewhat arbitrarily I chose a week of the Daily Lectionary from the *Lutheran Book of Worship*, namely Pentecost 5 of Year One.[3] From the texts for that week, I chose five that relate to the five themes and began each lecture with one of those texts. You'll have to decide whether this works or turns out to be eisegesis rather than exegesis.

As their titles indicate, the following lectures are about church music. As with lectures on any specific topic, these lectures bring with them the danger of making it seem as if music is the main thing. Music is very important in the life of the church, more important than is generally recognized, but it's not the main thing. The main thing could be construed in various ways. For purposes of this topic, which is broadly about what we do at worship, the main thing is the assembly of the church gathered around font, word, and table before the Trinity for the sake of the world. Music is the structural substance of the liturgy, of the song we sing around font, word, and table. It's very important, but it's not the main thing.

1 Which consists of extended glosses on Chapter 4, "The Heart of the Matter," in Paul Westermeyer, *The Church Musician*, rev. ed. (Augsburg Fortress, 1997), pp. 31–43, and the Daily Lectionary, Year One, Week of 5 Pentecost (rearranged within the week) in the *Lutheran Book of Worship* (Minneapolis: Augsburg Publishing House, 1978), p. 183.

2 See endnote 1 for the citation.

3 See endnote 1 for the citation.

Chapter 1

Church Music
as Praise

And David and all the house of Israel were making merry before
the Lord with all their might, with songs and lyres and harps and
tambourines and castanets and cymbals.

2 Samuel 6:5

The church's music is about the praise of God. David and the people
of Israel were carrying the ark of God, they sensed the presence of
God among them, and they made merry with music before the Lord.
They sang praise to God. This sentiment is not only expressed in
2 Samuel.[1] It is present throughout the Biblical narrative. It comes
to most obvious expression in the Psalms, as church musicians know
instinctively:

"Sing to the Lord a new song" (Psalm 98);
"Come into [God's] presence with singing" (Psalm 100);
"Let everything that breathes praise the Lord" (Psalm 150).

These imperatives make explicit what is implicit throughout the
Bible: God is to be praised, and music is one of the chief vehicles for
expressing that praise.

How does this come about? David and the people sense the

presence of God among them, and they make merry music before the Lord. Or as Martin Luther explained it from the church's characteristically Christological point of view,

> …God has cheered our hearts and minds through His dear Son, whom He gave for us to redeem us from sin, death, and the devil. [Anyone] who believes this earnestly cannot be quiet about it…[but] must gladly and willingly sing….[2]

God acts with loving-kindness toward us. We respond with a jubilant song of praise.

But what if we don't sense God's presence or loving-kindness among us? What if we can't fathom that God has done anything for us, or worse, that we think God has deserted us to our enemies? We are not the first people to be in this quandary. "My God, my God, why have you forsaken me?" cried the psalmist in Psalm 22. "Why don't you answer? You are holy, though I'm a worm. You took me from my mother's womb. From birth I'm cast on you. Yet I'm poured out like water, and evildoers surround me. Please don't be far away." And then without warning, in the midst of this nightmare, the psalmist switches course: "You have rescued me, and I will praise you."

Psalm 22 speaks to one kind of experience, certainly, but does it still beg the question? What if our experience is worse than Psalm 22? What if it's like Psalm 88? We cry to God, we're full of trouble, helpless, shunned by our companions, sensing only God's wrath, with darkness our only companion. There's no turn to praise as in Psalm 22. We finish the Psalm shut in by dread assaults, closed up with no exit. What then? Is Psalm 89 the response to Psalm 88? "I will sing of your steadfast love [and] proclaim your faithfulness to all generations," it begins. Does that provide the response? Do we simply sing the praise of God's faithfulness out of nowhere or out of what amounts to the same thing, the pit of our darkness?

Or is that the wrong question? Does the question need a broader scope? Is either our individual jubilation or our individual terror
before God too narrow? Is how we feel, no matter how good or how
bad, the measure and control of our praise? Or is the praise of God
fundamentally communal? Does praise of God itself stand outside of
our individual feelings? Is it the church's task as community to praise
God? We join individually when we can and as best as we can when
we can't. Is that why the text says not only that David made merry
with music before the Lord, but that David *and all the house of Israel*
did so?

Karl Barth, the Reformed theologian whose deep and detailed
writing does not necessarily call to mind musical expressions of
praise, highlights the communal aspect of the praise of God. He virtually made the church's song of praise a mark of the Christian
church.

> The praise of God which constitutes the community and its
> assemblies seeks to bind and commit and therefore to be
> expressed, to well up and be sung in concert. The Christian
> community sings. It is not a choral society. Its singing is not
> a concert. But from inner, material necessity it sings.
> Singing is the highest form of human expression. It is to
> such supreme expression that the *vox humana* is devoted in
> the ministry of the Christian community....
>
> What we can and must say quite confidently is that the
> community which does not sing is not the community. And
> where it cannot sing in living speech, or only archaically in
> repetition of the modes and texts of the past; where it does
> not sing but sighs and mumbles spasmodically, shamefaced-
> ly and with an ill grace, it can be at best only a troubled
> community which is not sure of its cause and of whose min-
> istry and witness there can be no great expectation.[3] In
> these circumstances it has every reason to pray that this gift

which is obviously lacking or enjoyed only in sparing meas-ure will be granted afresh and more generously lest all the other members suffer. The praise of God which finds its concrete culmination in the singing of the community is one of the indispensable basic forms of the ministry of the community.[4]

But there are times when even a whole community can't sing. In the face of the Holocaust, a whole people or at least whole communities of that people were silenced. Just as rape silences the individual, so rape of a community silences a people. And then what? The praise of God goes on. The people of God elsewhere sing it in agony and pain with those who can't sing.

The scope is broader still. The Psalm says, "Let everything that breathes praise the Lord." "Everything that breathes" means the whole creation. The song of praise is there from the beginning of cre-ation. It's what we sing with the whole creation as the people of God. When the foundations of the earth were laid, already then the morn-ing stars sang together and all the children of God shouted for joy (Job 38:4–6). We could say God's praise is a duty of the whole creation, a delightful duty even when we can't sense the delight, even at times of deepest despair when someone else stands in and sings for us. The song of praise goes on with us and without us.

There is a deep mystery here, the mystery of praising the Triune name. That is why superficial talk about praise of God and superfi-cial music associated with such trivial talk is so enervating and silly. Whatever we may say about this, the church's song of praise is not frivolous. It's an essential part of the church's being and our being as members of Christ's body, related to the being of God and to the being of the universe. It's not something we can add on, as if we could sew a patch onto a pre-existent garment. It's part of the garment of the whole creation, intrinsic to the creation.

It's not only imbedded in the creation's physical being from the beginning. It's also imbedded in the being and telos of time. Praise of God is the point toward which the whole creation is moving, as Patrick Miller has said.[5] The organization of the Psalter toward everything that breathes singing a song of praise to God is not just a rhetorical device. It's a proleptic reality. It's where the cosmos is headed. Praise of God, to say the least, is no small thing and, therefore, worth doing well. At its heart, praise takes musical form. It's the music of the spheres, the music of the church in its assemblies in community, and our individual songs in concert with all the rest. The *music* of praise is also worth doing well.

+ + +

So, then, David and the people sense God's presence and make merry before the Lord. God "[cheers] our hearts and minds," and we sing with jubilant abandon. From "inner, material necessity" the church sings, even when everything is against us and we are not cheered. The song of praise is imbedded in the whole creation and is its goal.

Though that's a complicated mystery in one sense, in another sense it's too simple for us. To do it does not take complex thought. The thought comes after the doing and reflects on the doing. The doing is reflexive rather than reflective. The doing is like small children singing, as Anne Lamott says, because "they haven't made the separation between speech and music."[6] However, rather than becoming like children and just doing the most natural thing, we like to tie ourselves in knots about it. That way we can stare at ourselves and avoid both the song of praise and the Triune God to whom it is directed. So, for example, we are now in a period of history when we love to attack ourselves for not praising God the way others do. The grass is always greener on the other side of the street, it would seem, or political correctness demands a certain style. We don't move

15

enough. We don't clap enough. We don't sing loudly enough. We don't use the right styles. We aren't sincere enough. We aren't this, we aren't that, we aren't the other thing, we don't do this, we don't do that, we don't do the other thing.

It's instructive that there is nothing about stylistic correctness or proper piety in the account of David and the people. They sang unselfconsciously in their style "with songs and lyres and harps and tambourines and castanets and cymbals." They also sang "with all their might." That's the closest we get to proper piety, and we should learn from it, but it still doesn't tell you a whole lot. People express "all their might" in quite different ways. One can imagine the Israelites in all their manifold differences much the same as a Jewish synagogue today where an exceedingly wide variety of pieties are likely to be expressed simultaneously with more or less vigorous gestures.

There is nothing about stylistic correctness or proper piety in the quotation from Luther. Just "gladly and willingly sing," he says. There is nothing about stylistic correctness or proper piety in the quotation from Karl Barth, unless archaic repetition or spasmodic and shamefaced mumbling are mistaken for marks of style or piety rather than faith. From "inner, material necessity" the church simply sings. There's nothing about stylistic correctness or proper piety in Job's account. The morning stars simply sang together, and all the children of God shouted for joy.

Are we to doubt that the song of Israel was a song of praise to God? Are we to doubt that Lutherans have praised God in their song? Are we to doubt that Reformed communities have praised God in theirs, or Orthodox or Episcopal or Roman Catholic communities in theirs? Are we to doubt that the morning stars and children of God praised God in their song? Did (does) the music of the church's various communities all sound the same? Did (do) postures and gestures all look the same? Hardly. Except for operating within the created order of the harmonic series, they are quite different. Did (does) stylistic correctness or proper piety make one of those communities more or less worthy than the other ones? Hardly.

What, pray tell, is wrong with an anthem by Thomas Tallis that praises God? What is wrong with a motet by Palestrina that praises God or an ostinato led by Patrick Matsikenyiri in Zimbabwe? What is wrong with a setting of a Psalm by Ralph Vaughan Williams or an organ improvisation by Gerre Hancock that gives praise to God? Why should any of these be attacked any more than they should be affirmed at the expense of other styles? What is wrong with the small congregation who, having no instruments or choir, sings a unison psalm tone or the Ordinary of the Mass or a canticle at Evening Prayer or a hymn—all without any instrumental or choral assistance? What is wrong with a Methodist hymn-sing? What is wrong with a choir that sings a glorious and well-rehearsed *Sanctus* on the people's behalf? What is wrong with I-to Loh or Pablo Sosa or Messiaen or Penderecki or Stravinsky or John Tavener or Arvo Pärt? What is wrong with the congregation who moves vigorously when it sings? What is wrong with one who sings with little movement and much meditative shalom? What is wrong with black gospel or Taizé? In short, what is wrong with singing songs of praise to God in the language of one's skill and capacity, in the style appropriate to a given people in a specific time and place?

We could ask the question another way. What choice do we have? If we sing from inner, material necessity, we will naturally do it as ably as possible, in whatever state we find ourselves, with whatever resources we have and can assemble, and with mutual help for and from one another.

Let us cease, then, to lambaste ourselves with needless, pointless, foolish, and counterproductive self-inflicted pain about the politically or piously correct "how" of our song. That does little more than silence us. Let us simply sing and keep figuring out the how as we go along. Let us be aware of the varied musical styles the human race has produced within the common created order of sound, bold enough to affirm that ours is one of them with its own validity and that neither ours nor the other ones are to be despised. They are all to be cherished and affirmed, *ours included*. Let us sing the praise of God as ably as possible in our style, aware of, enhanced by, and put in perspective by our sisters and brothers in other styles.

+ + +

It's easy enough to say all that. Doing it requires some work. No music in any style simply appears. Composing has to be done. Choices have to be made. Someone has to lead the people's praise. To be expressed, the musical response of praise for God's grace needs form and shape. Someone has to take responsibility for that forming and shaping.

This is the delightful vocation of the church musician—the person whom I prefer to call the cantor, the chief singer among the body of singers, the one fundamentally responsible for the congregation's song and for all the choral and instrumental music that surrounds it or grows out of it. The church musician has to sense the capacities and resources of a particular people, then write or choose music that expresses the praise of God with those peculiar capacities and resources. Once the music is composed or chosen, the church musician is the one who must then lead the congregation's peculiar people in actually singing the song of praise.

What does this mean? Many things, including these:

1. The song of praise that your congregation makes is the most excellent, no matter what its makeup. That is, the song of praise is the people's office. It requires their voices, not canned voices piped in by some nightmare of surrogate virtual reality.
2. The song of praise is preeminently vocal. Words are the means

by which our praise is articulated, and music is the means by which the articulation is carried aloft so that song gives wings to the words.

3. But, as I indicated before, not only humanity sings this song of praise. The whole creation is called to join in. Or, better perhaps, we are called to join the whole creation in its song of praise. Wordless instruments reflect the song of creation and are, therefore, called to play their part. That part is not only to accompany the voices, but to sound alone where fitting and appropriate. Their sounding is not an afterthought or an unrelated addendum any more than the vocal sounding is. The whole song of praise is woven into the created order from its inception to its consummation.

1 See also the duplicate passage in 1 Chronicles 13:8, the only difference being that "song" is singular rather than plural.

2 Martin Luther, "Preface to the Baptist Hymnal, 1545," *Luther's Works, Volume 53, Liturgy and Hymns,* ed. Ulrich S. Leupold (Philadelphia: Fortress Press, 1965), p. 333.

3 Barth encodes here the bane and blessing of the Reformed position. The bane is the difficulty of understanding the value of human habit, a knee-jerk reaction against catholicity, and a sectarian tendency; the blessing is the reminder that the church is always in need of reformation, always reforming, and that each new generation needs to embrace the faith with renewed vitality.

4 Karl Barth, *Church Dogmatics,* IV, Part Three, Second Half, trans. G. W. Bromiley (Edinburgh: T. & T. Clark, 1962), pp. 866–867.

5 Patrick Miller, "The Psalms as Praise and Poetry," *The Hymn* 40:4 (October 1989), 13.

6 Anne Lamott, *Traveling Mercies* (New York: Anchor Books, 2000), p. 66.

Chapter 2

Church Music as Prayer

I cry with my voice to the Lord. With my voice I make
supplication to the Lord.

Psalm 142:1

The church's music is about prayer to God. With the psalmist, the
church cries out to God and makes supplication with musical pat-
terns and cadences, with rhythmic ebb and flow. If our delightful
song of praise is at times an anguished groan, our song of prayer is
more characteristically a lament. But our prayer is not all crying out
of the depths with tears of pain. As our praise can be anguished, so
our prayer can be jubilant. Our liturgies themselves are prayer or,
more accurately, in them praise and prayer come together in a
curious and wondrous multi-valent combination.

Take *Kyrie eleison*, for example. It is often viewed, especially in
its English translation, as a penitential plea. So it sometimes appears
in penitential rites as a response to a litany of our faults or as a
symbol of our misery between a confession and an absolution.

That is probably a misuse of the *Kyrie*, or at least not its original
or more intrinsic meaning. Its more characteristic use in the early
church as part of the deacon's litany gives it the quality of a football

cheer—"Lord, you are the one who has mercy." The deacon bids the people, "Let us pray to the Lord," and the people respond not with a penitential plea but with, "Lord, you are the one who has mercy." J-Glenn Murray, Director of the Office of Pastoral Liturgy for the Diocese of Cleveland, explained the *Kyrie's* meaning even better.[1] "If you went to a 103-year-old African American woman," he said, "and told her she had just won $10 million and she raised her hands and shouted 'Lord, have mercy,' that's what it means." Praise and prayer run together.

+ + +

The roots of our worship in temple and synagogue are sung prayer. The church's chant, in its various eastern or western forms, is often viewed as an envelope for prayer if not actual prayer. Joseph Gajard, for example, sees Gregorian chant as prayer itself.[2] The Solesmes school of thought even calls Gregorian chant "a way of reaching up to God" and "a means of sanctification."[3]

Those who live in the heritage of the sixteenth century Reformers are likely to wince at such a perspective because it can be twisted into a hopeless search for musical merit as the means to get us into God's presence. Such a twist is a perversion, probably not Solesmes' intent, and not the essence of music's relation to prayer. The church bears witness to a healthier perspective throughout its history, including its history where some may not expect it, from the Reformation onward. John Calvin considered church music in the section on Prayer in his *Institutes.*[4] In keeping with the whole church catholic, Luther and the Lutheran Church has sung collects and indeed the whole liturgy. A large body of the church's hymns, even from sources where the liturgy has not characteristically been sung, are sung prayers.

Though the emphasis may differ, almost all traditions treat music as prayer or in some way related to prayer. That should not surprise us any more than music's relation to praise should surprise us. Human beings both laugh and weep. Laughter is the incipient form of sung praise, as weeping is the incipient form of sung prayer.[5] The two very often run into one another and cross.[6] That is why we find ourselves weeping when we laugh and laughing when we weep. And that is why at worship we cannot always sort out whether our song is praise, prayer, or both.

Though we cannot, and should not, try to sort out in the doing whether our song is praise, prayer, or both, we can and should sort it out when we seek understanding. Psalm 142 helps our understanding. "I cry to the Lord," says the psalmist. "I pour out my complaint and show God my trouble. What's the trouble? My spirit was overwhelmed. You knew my path, but they have laid a snare."

Here we come upon this "they," this enemy who is forever plaguing the psalmist, who always remains undefined. The psalmist, of course, is not alone in isolating this "they." That's one reason these ancient songs keep ringing true. This enemy forever plagues us too, as in the hymn "Come, Labor On."[7] We have some sense of how to define the enemy in our own lives with more precision than the generality of the Psalm, but not quite enough to make the definition complete or neat. We know who is out to get us sometimes. We sometimes know who hates us and whom we hate. We know about the forces of disease, sometimes the quite specific ones that snare us. We know about social evils before which we seem to fall powerless. That is, we can isolate this or that evil "they" at numerous points in our lives. Taken as a whole, however, these "theys" form a less-than-clear but nevertheless palpable evil out there that is arrayed against us. We find ourselves in its clutches. We look for help on our right hand, but nobody knows us. Nobody seems to care. All human refuge fails. Nobody cares for our soul.

So we cry to God and say, "You are my refuge and my portion in the land of the living. Hear my cry, for I am brought very low. Deliver me from my persecutors because they are stronger than I. Bring my soul out of prison, so that I may praise your name, so that the righteous may compass me about." Underneath the cry of pain is the ancient expectation that God will deal bountifully with us.

Something like that is the nature of our lamentation, our prayer. But it's not the only thing our prayer is concerned about. At worship we cry out in our need, but we also cry out for others, as I Timothy instructs us. "I exhort therefore," he says, "that, first of all, supplications, prayers, intercessions, *and* giving of thanks, be made for all people" (I Timothy 2:1). In our eucharistic assemblies, we try to follow Timothy's instruction week in and week out. We intercede for all people in their need. Our worship is for the life of the world, to quote Alexander Schmemann.[8] It is not an ingrown activity where we stare at our own needs. Our doors are open to the world, and we pray for the needs of all. We intercede for others. So we rightly have lengthy lists of prayer requests that are central to our being as church. We live for the life of the world, and we encompass the needs of others in our petitions to God.

Note that we also give thanks. Not all prayer is lamentation. Giving thanks is also welcome. Not only welcome, but intrinsic to our prayer. Expressions of joy are not only about praise, though they may move there. But in our prayers themselves we give thanks for all people, for one another, for all creation, for our preservation and redemption, for the gifts that grace our daily living, for small things we overlook in our headlong rush, for meditative shalom, for healing. The list goes on and on. Once we begin, our list spills out in endless profusion. In our public assemblies, some restraint is in order in its expression. Individually, there is a place for more abandon. But we should not overlook thanksgiving in either context.

We also pray for all in authority, as Timothy instructs us

(I Timothy 2:2), "that all may lead a quiet and peaceable life in all godliness and honesty." Our prayer is not only for others' needs. It's not only thanksgiving. It's also intercession for those in authority. We pray that the common good may be served, that civil communities may live together in peace and harmony. Once again, we have doors open to the world. We live for the life of the world, and we intercede for the common good and those who make decisions about it.

+ + +

What does any of this have to do with music? Many things, including these:

1. The wail of lamentation goes beyond speech. Speech can't carry the moan. The cry comes out in incipient musical form. It doesn't come out in words to which we add music. It comes out in a musical flow, which we craft. It comes out in a musical cry of pain, which we have to work on if it is to have any longevity beyond the initial moan. So, for example, Paul Manz is in a hospital waiting to hear if his son John will live or die. He doesn't speak, "E'en so, Lord Jesus, quickly come." He sings it (internally? externally?) and then, with help from his wife Ruth who adapts Revelation 22, writes out its implications into an anthem that we all share thereafter. Or, as in the case of the death of Nicholas and Claire Wolterstorff's son Eric, the "cold burning pain. . .'the wave cry, the wind cry'"[9] of the parents finds musical expression in the commission given to the composer Cary Ratcliff.[10]

    The point here is not that every piece has to come out of such specific suffering or grief. Composers who have no tragedy in their own lives, if that could be imagined, can enter into the pain and suffering of the human race and articulate our prayers of lamentation quite well. The point is that the moan of our pain is at heart musical and that, like all our musical activity, it takes shaping by a craftsperson after the initial cry has been voiced.

2. Responses like "Hear our prayer" are musical. We sing them. We sing them even when we think we speak them because the communal cry to God is incipiently and inherently musical in actual shape and flow. Even when the congregation seems to speak a response, there is melody and rhythm in it. We breathe together. In the case of "Hear our prayer," the congregation's pitch is likely to move downward from the initial word "Hear" to the final word "prayer." The brief but insistent plea is likely to take a rhythmic shape that matches the import of the words.

   What I mean to say here extends beyond this simple response. Any communal vocal sounds the congregation makes are inherently musical. They can, of course, be composed and then become more obviously musical. My point is that what is not obviously musical is itself, at the very least, incipiently musical and that the congregation's prayer is imbedded in and grows out of this primal music. No assembly at prayer can avoid this reality.

3. To pray for those in authority, to cry out to God in our prayer for the needs of the world is to voice one of the church's central concerns, namely, that in our communities in this world people may live together in peace and harmony, with justice. Notice that we blithely say "peace and harmony," usually without thinking of the musical implications. Our music *and* its harmony—that is, our singing together as the body of Christ in prayer at worship in what we broadly call "harmony," which may be "in harmony" or in unison—is a sign of our societal harmony.

This is not just my idea. It has an ancient lineage. Albert Blackwell recently cited it in the Roman general Scipio, Augustine

who leans on Scipio, Jonathon Edwards, and Shakespeare. Here's
Augustine.

> In the case of music for strings or winds, and in vocal music,
> there is a certain harmony to be kept between different
> parts, and if this is altered or disorganised the cultivated ear
> finds it intolerable; and the united efforts of dissimilar voic-
> es are blended into harmony by the exercise of restraint. In
> the same way a community of different classes, high, low,
> and middle, unites, like the varying sounds of music, to form
> harmony of very different parts through the exercise of
> rational restraint; and what is called harmony in music
> answers to concord in a community, and it is the best
> and closest bond of security in a country. And this cannot
> possibly exist without justice.[11]

And here's Jonathon Edwards.

> The best, most beautiful, and most perfect way that we have
> of expressing sweet concord of mind to each other, is by
> music. When I would form in my mind an idea of a society
> in the highest degree happy, I think of them as expressing
> their love, their joy, and the inward concord and spiritual
> beauty of their souls by sweetly singing to each other.[12]

Our musical divisions reflect our societal divisions. Our singing
together in our worshiping assemblies reflects the counter-cultural
peace, harmony, and justice the church seeks and the restraint we
have to exercise in their pursuit. Singing together in our assemblies
of worship is no small matter. Church music grows out of our prayer
and has enormous implications for our life together.

+ + +

As for leading the people's praise, there is also work to do for the church musician in leading the people's prayer. The cantor can lead the people's praise alone, but in leading the people's prayer the cantor plays more of a dialogical role with the clergy and other leaders at worship. The presiding and assisting ministers usually bear the primary responsibility for the proper prayers and petitions of a particular service. In some sense, the clergy bears the ultimate responsibility for the prayer life of a people, though the laity and not the clergy are usually the most reliable bearers of prayer in any congregation. Assuming the composing and choosing we have already denoted, the cantor assists the community at prayer in these ways.

First, the cantor provides the leadership for the people's litanic responses, spoken and sung. Corporate responses to bids, even when spoken, as I have indicated, are incipiently musical, that is, elated communal forms of speech. The cantor through his or her direct leadership or through training of the choir helps shape this response as may be necessary (communities often do this with little or no help) and thereby helps to shape the prayer life of the people.

Second, since some hymns are themselves prayers, the cantor leads the people in prayer by leading hymns. This is straightforward and obvious, but it takes considerable thought and effort if it is to be carried out faithfully and well. Prayers take many forms, from lamentations and supplications to thanksgivings and intercessions for the common good. One musical envelope does not fit all of these forms, any more than one musical envelope makes sense of the many musical styles and performance practices that musicians are required to learn.

Third, the choir sings texts that are prayers. In this case, the cantor leads a group who prays on behalf of the people just as the presider or assisting minister does. This is obviously not a performance *before* the people; it is instead an act of intercession *for and with* the people—which makes applause in this instance very strange and thoroughly unwelcome.

1 At the *Worship 2000 Jubilee* of the Evangelical Lutheran Church in America in Chicago at Navy Pier, July 10, 2000.

2 Dom Joseph Gajard, *The Solesmes Method*, trans. R. Cecile Gabain (Collegeville: The Liturgical Press, 1960), p. vii.

3 Ibid., p. 85.

4 John Calvin, *Institutes of the Christian Religion*, ed. John T. McNeill (Philadelphia: Westminster Press, 1960) III: xx: 31–32.

5 Cf. Joseph Gelineau, *Voices and Instruments in Christian Worship* (Collegeville: The Liturgical Press, 1964), pp. 15–19.

6 For a very helpful discussion of the primal nature and close relation of prayer and praise, as well as their relation to thanksgiving and proclamation, see Patrick D. Miller, Jr., *Interpreting the Psalms*, (Philadelphia: Fortress Press, 1986), pp. 64–78.

7 *The [Episcopal] Hymnal 1982* (New York: The Church Hymnal Corporation, 1985), no. 541, st. 2.

8 Alexander Schmemann, *For the Life of the World: Sacraments and Orthodoxy* (St. Vladimir's Seminary Press, 1973).

9 Nicholas Wolterstorff, *Lament for a Son* (Grand Rapids: William B. Eerdmans Publishing Company, 1987), pp. 9 and 103.

10 Ibid., p. 105.

11 Quoted from Augustine, *City of God* 2.21, 72, from Scipio's *De republica* 2.42f., in Albert Blackwell, *The Sacred in Music* (Louisville: Westminster John Knox Press, 1999), p. 189.

12 Quoted from Jonathon Edwards' Miscellany # 188, *The "Miscellanies,"* 331, in Blackwell, p. 189.

Chapter 3

Church Music as Proclamation

And when he had given him leave, Paul, standing on the steps
motioned with his hand to the people; and when there was a
great hush, he spoke to them in the Hebrew language.

Acts 21:40

Preaching grows out of silence. It begins after a hush. It requires
sounds that are shaped into intelligible words, against the backdrop
of silence so they can be heard. Preachers utter intelligible vocables
in the hope that they will be heard beyond their human words as the
word of God in this place to this people, so that we will know
again—or perhaps for the first time—that we are adopted as daugh-
ters and sons, that we are graced and loved beyond all imagining by
the power behind the cosmos known in Christ and presented to us
by the Holy Spirit.

The church's music is also about proclamation. It, too, is heard
against a backdrop of silence. It, too, requires intelligible vocables,
but this time they are borne and broken open by music. As Luther
might say, the Word of God is proclaimed in words, and wonder of
wonders, words about the Word of God can be sung. The author of
Ephesians was aware of this same wonder.

...but be filled with the Spirit, addressing one another in psalms
and hymns and spiritual songs...

Ephesians 5:18b–19a

Here it is clear that music is a means by which the words and Word
of the Gospel are proclaimed. Luther referred to the parallel verse in
Colossians (3:16) and wrote,

...St. Paul...exhorted the Colossians to sing spiritual songs
and psalms heartily unto the Lord so that God's word and
Christian teaching might be instilled and implanted in
many ways.[1]

There is often a legitimate element of praise in thoughts of this
sort. As Carl Schalk has said,

"God is praised when the Gospel is proclaimed; and the
proclamation of the Gospel is the way Christians rightly
praise God. There is no artificial division between songs that
'proclaim' and songs that 'praise.' For unless 'praise songs'
proclaim the good news of the Gospel they are not, in the
Christian sense, praise songs at all."[2]

One can easily move, therefore, from music as proclamation to music
as praise without realizing it. Such a natural leap removes the
distinction between these two motifs and tends to collapse one into
the other. Usually, since praise is so obvious, it takes precedence.

Schalk is right that there is no artificial distinction between the
two motifs, at least at the level of practice. However, for logical and
theological clarity, and to do justice to the church's musical heritage,
music's responsibility to proclaim the word needs to be kept separate,
even though the connections to praise can be close. Much of the
church's musical heritage is exegetical or proclamatory. Music
proclaims, interprets, breaks open the Word of God. Here are three
ways that this is true.

1. When the congregation sings, it proclaims the gospel to itself as a whole, to its individual members, and to anyone who may overhear it. We address one another in "psalms and hymns and spiritual songs." In the process, we often find that William Cowper articulated what we would say if we could have said it as well as he did. Though it's difficult to sing his hymn anymore as it stands because of its masculine pronouns, it nonetheless expresses a basic Christian experience.

> Sometimes a light surprises
> > The Christian while he sings;
> It is the Lord who rises
> > With healing in His wings.[3]

2. Music has been employed to proclaim texts from ancient times. That is why, until recently in the last several centuries, Biblical lessons have almost invariably been sung or chanted. The singing not only amplifies them. More profoundly, it breaks them open so that we can hear them with potency and power.

   The declamation of texts leads to preaching that itself is more or less musical, depending on the tradition. "Pulpit tones" illustrate this, often negatively. So do the dialogical utterances of a black Baptist preacher and congregation that may start with what sounds like speech and gradually break into song. The same thing happens with a horse race or an auction on a much less profound level. What starts as speech becomes more and more melodic and more and more rhythmic as the race or the auction proceeds. To announce something or to declaim any text is musical by its very nature.

3. Motets by Schütz, chorale preludes, cantatas, and Passions by Bach, and numerous compositions by other composers are more complex examples of the same intent. Without a

"kerygmatic" (proclamatory) understanding of these pieces, they are incomprehensible.[4] They may work for concerts in some purely musical sense, but they only really come alive when they are placed in their native soil as proclamation in the context of a worshiping assembly.

How does this work itself out for the church musician's vocation? Here are two ways.

1. The cantor aids the readers in the proclamatory work of reading lessons. This may on some occasions involve the use of more or less complex choral or solo musical settings of lessons in place of readings. That is rare for most of us. It should not be normative, although it deserves more consideration than we normally accord it. Where lessons are sung by a lector, the cantor should obviously aid those who do the singing. For most of us, lessons are read. There, too, the musician has a role we rarely think about, namely, helping readers read clearly. Musicians are among those who need to understand phrasing and the ebb and flow of a line of words. Choral musicians need to understand diction and enunciation. These are necessities in good reading, which is close to becoming a lost art in many churches and in the culture at large. Musicians can help repair the breach so that lessons can be understood.

2. The preacher has the primary proclamatory task of publishing the good news of God's grace and love among us. As I indicated earlier, by careful application to the Biblical word and the daily newspaper, the preacher speaks his or her poor human words in the hope that they will be heard as the Word of God itself so that the love of God in Christ will be known among us.

The cantor cannot and should not attempt to "preach" in the same way the preacher does. This is because the composing of text and music and the preparation of music by musicians preclude the preacher's relevance to the moment, and because the preacher can examine detailed relationships in spoken prose in a way that is not possible for the musician.

On the other hand, an anthem or some other piece by the choir can be proclamatory in a way the preacher cannot proclaim. This is related not simply to the power of music to exegete a text with melodies or rhythms that open up its meaning. This is related more profoundly to music's polyphonic potential. A polyphonic piece of music or the simultaneous juxtaposition of two texts gives the musician an opportunity to proclaim relationships in a way that is not open to the preacher, who must communicate in a stream of monologue.

One of the most striking examples of this polyphonic opportunity is found in the last chorus of J. S. Bach's *Christmas Oratorio*. There, trumpets and timpani are joined to the tune associated with "O Sacred Head, Now Wounded," set now, however, to a Christus Victor text about sin and death being conquered—all sung around the manger. No preacher can join Christmas, Lent, and Easter in such a proclamation as Bach did there.

The basic point here is that the relevance of the moment is not the responsibility of music, which is of necessity more prepared and formal. Rather, music has the capacity for breaking open the gospel in a way spoken words cannot, by giving a broader scope and context.

+ + +

What we are discussing here is related to a topic I was assigned recently by the National Association of Pastoral Musicians at a meeting in Orlando, Florida. I need to repeat two points I made then.

The first is the thinking that music's proclamatory character should lead us to be preachy which, in turn, means that we write or choose what is poorly crafted, pseudo, banal, and inane. We do this on the premise that a lowest common denominator kitsch will have some universal appeal. It may or may not have momentary appeal, but sooner or later—and sooner than we think—it will collapse in on itself because of its lack of substance and incapacity for repetition. Whether it collapses is not the central problem, however. The central temptation here is dishonesty. Whatever we are about in the life of the church, its musical life included, we are certainly about honesty and integrity, not cheap tricks or dishonest kitsch. Such music is not worthy of our people and surely does not exegete any of the powerful texts we have to sing. It does little more than trivialize our proclamation into an ingrown address to ourselves.

The second issue can be phrased as a question. What does it mean musically to exegete a text? Beyond music's polyphonic potential, what does it mean? Are we talking about program music, absolute music, word painting, a baroque understanding of musical conventions, a subterranean system of number symbolism, a romantic haze that can't be defined, Messiaen's language with a musical alphabet and bird song, or what? Does music do for texts what Paul Nelson says stained glass does for light? He says medieval stained glass is not about telling Biblical stories, notwithstanding what we have been wrongly told. The windows, he says, are far too complex and far away to do that. Stained glass is about light transformed into emblems of grace. He suggests that something like that is what music does for texts. Does music do these things? The answer is probably any one of them, or some of them, or all of them, or perhaps none of them or something else, depending on when and where. Perhaps we do better to point to examples of texts being broken open musically, from which we can learn:

- a motet on a text from Romans by Heinrich Schütz;
- a southern white folk hymn;

- a certain setting of the Ordinary;
- a setting of a Psalm by Stravinsky;
- hymn tunes from England, Argentina, Manila, Germany;
- an anthem by Orlando Gibbons;
- a black spiritual;
- a certain setting of the *Magnificat* or *Nunc Dimittis*;
- a piece from the Iona Community;
- one from Taizé;
- a certain chant;
- a certain antiphon;
- Brahms's German Requiem;
- an organ suite by Messiaen;
- a cantata or a Passion by Bach.

These and other musical examples are helpful, but the question remains whether we can say anything more generally about how music breaks open a text? Maybe, but it will be tantalizingly incomplete and untidily fecund. In the book I cited earlier, Albert Blackwell[5] (a university professor who serves an Episcopal church as their musician) says that we live in the universe God created. For sound, that means the universe of the harmonic series. Without embracing a medieval posture of cosmic harmony, he nevertheless wants to say that deconstructionists who argue that there is absolutely no meaning in music other than momentary cultural constructs are wrong. He thinks there is something in our music that "transcends contingency." God's created order of the harmonic series embraces all our musical systems, he says, and there is both quality and the "potentially sacramental" in some music, notably (but not only) Mozart, of course.

Blackwell's position is not without its problems, but it can't be summarily dismissed either. To apply it to music's proclamatory responsibility leads one to say that absolute music does not mean anything, but a Phrygian melody nevertheless "means" something different from a melody in a major key, especially when joined with a text. Neither you nor I can plummet this mystery, but as musicians we know it. We live in it. Its paradox can be stated like this: music that best breaks open a text has to be able to stand on its own, like the best Gregorian chant or a piece by J. S. Bach, without the text to support it. A second paradox follows: different musical lenses which themselves "mean" something yet don't mean anything will make the text mean different things.

---

1 Martin Luther, "Preface to the Wittenberg Hymnal, 1524," *Luther's Works*, Vol. 53, p. 316.

2 Carl Schalk, "The Church and the Composer," *Cross Accent* 8:1 (Spring 2000): 4.

3 William Cowper (1731–1800).

4 See Robin A. Leaver, "The Liturgical Place and Homiletic Purpose of Bach's Cantatas," *Worship*, 59: 3 (May 1985): 194–202, and Robin A. Leaver, *J.S. Bach as Preacher: His Passions and Music in Worship* (St. Louis: Concordia Publishing House, 1984).

5 Albert L. Blackwell, *The Sacred in Music* (Louisville: Westminster John Knox Press, 1999).

Chapter 4

Church Music as Story

Blessed be the Lord God of Israel, for he has visited and redeemed his people.

Luke 1:68

Praise, prayer, and proclamation for many probably move from the most to the least obvious definitions of church music. A still less obvious aspect of the church's song is, upon reflection, both the most obvious and the most profound: the church's song is about the story. "Blessed be the God of Israel," we sing. This and the other canticles are the texts we most characteristically sing. And what do they do? They tell the story.

When the people of God recount the history of God's mighty acts, they invariably sing. We note again that at the creation the morning stars "sang together" (Job 38:7). Thereafter, at all the important points of articulation in the story there is song. For example, after their deliverance from Egypt, Miriam, Moses, and the people sang a song (Exod. 25:1–8). When David prepared a place for the ark, he appointed musicians who sang a song of thanksgiving (I Chronicles 16:8–34). At Christ's birth there is song (Luke 2:14). At the consummation there is song (throughout the book of Revelation).

The reason for the psalmists' songs of praise is that God "has done marvelous things" (Ps. 98:10). There is a story to sing, a reason for the praise. New Testament canticles, like the *Magnificat* (Luke 1:47–55) and the *Benedictus* (Luke 1:68–79), are songs that recount God's mighty deeds just like the Psalms, but now with an explicit Christocentric note. The songs of Revelation tell the story of God's mighty acts in an eschatological frame of reference. From the beginning of the Biblical saga to its end, from one end of history to the other, the story is a song to be sung.

The same can be said of the church's hymnody. It is partly praise, prayer, and proclamation, to be sure. But it is perhaps more profoundly story. If you lay out the hymns of almost any standard hymnal in a sequential fashion, you find the entire story of God's mighty acts there—from creation through Old Testament history to Christ's incarnation to church in the world "between the times" to last things. Individual hymns often tell the story by themselves. "O Love, How Deep, How Broad, How High"[1] is a good example. Music is the vehicle by which the community remembers and celebrates what God has done, which leads to three points about the church's song as story.

First, it is sequentially and logically easy to lay out the story of the Bible from creation to consummation as I have just done. In fact, the story is more sophisticated than that, and sorting it out is more complicated. Like our own stories and those of the psalmist, it often begins in the midst of things with personal laments and personal songs of thanksgiving, and with people who emerge on the stage of history with their own struggles and visions. We all have obvious or less obvious calls to our vocations, which we manage over time to sort out. Sometimes we don't understand them until well after the fact. For the Christian, the event of Jesus stands at the center of the story and is its key. It radically alters and fulfills all our personal laments, thanksgivings, struggles, and visions, and gradually gives meaning to past and present.

Second, music has a peculiar communal and mnemonic charac-ter. We sing to recall and retell our story. We sing our ballads, if you will. A group who sings together becomes one and remembers its story, and therefore who it is, in a particularly potent way. Hitler knew and exploited the demonic potential of that reality. Whenever the church loses or neglects to sing its song, a vacuum is created, which the Hitlers among us will invariably fill.

Third, music spins itself out through time just like the story that the song recounts and just like worship where the song is sung. As the Eastern Orthodox church knows so well, music "is by nature an event. It is dynamic rather than fixed." Like the story and like wor-ship and "more than any other art…it carries the possibility of change, of transformation."[2] This means it is peculiarly suited not only to tell the story, but to accompany worship as well because worship also moves through time and is in fact about transformation through the paschal mystery. This probably is most obvious at the Easter Vigil, but it's there at every paschal feast and every prayer office as well.

+ + +

What is the musician's role in relation to the story? There are two categories here, one related to the story itself and the other related more broadly to time.

1. The cantor helps the people sing the whole story and thereby tells the story. The preacher also tells the story, of course, as does the teacher. Some understandings of preaching would even argue that it is at heart storytelling. There is a sense in which that is true: proclaiming the good news is telling the story of God's love. But the preacher is always compelled to apply the story to us in this moment so that the searing edge

of God's love can burn its way into our hearts. This requires the context of the whole story, and preaching can only give that context over time or in an ancillary way. The cantor is more specifically responsible for the context and the fullness of the story. (This is related to the difference between the preacher's and the church musician's role in proclamation, but here I have in mind not proclamation so much as narrative or ballad.)

This means the cantor tells the story by seeing to it that the whole story is sung. The lessons, prayers, and sermon for a given service are likely to have a thematic focus. The hymnody, psalmody, and anthems ought to relate to that focus also, but in addition they flesh out the rest of the story and remind us of other parts of the plot. Over the course of a year, the whole story should certainly have been sung, from creation to last things. This means that doing the same six or ten hymns over and over does not serve the people well; it keeps them from singing the whole story and omits much of the context the preacher requires for his or her words.

Let me expand this just a bit by focusing on some problems of our culture in relation to the story and memory. We need to consider the cluster of music, memory, and story with some thoughtful care.

Part of the problem of our limited memory bank can be attributed to neglect, though liturgical churches are fortunate at this point because the liturgy protects us from ourselves and keeps the whole story before us even when we are apt to forget it or those pieces of it we find less palatable. Even in the liturgical churches, we have probably not tended to the story as well as we ought to have. Fair enough. But the problem goes deeper than neglect. There are voices in the last several decades who have been arguing for doing all throw-away music, who have essentially been saying that memory doesn't matter. Not only that, but for legitimate reasons of justice and the vernacular, we have been revising our texts over and over again. We need to do that, of course, but we have often done it without regard to the church catholic so that we now have various versions of liturgical texts, hymns, and prayers in all our hymnals and no common memory bank to draw from. And no Bishop Thomas Cranmer has as yet appeared among us to give us durable language appropriate to worship the way he did so ably.

When you add the doomsayers and Calamity Janes among us who believe that only their newest schemes will save us, you get a perspective that says junk everything and start from scratch. If you add to that a culture that is Biblically illiterate and you do nothing in the church to counter these tendencies, you wind up with no memory at all. Even if the Hitlers don't fill the vacuum, we still wind up with communal Alzheimer's disease—no memory, no way to put the pieces together. What happens to individuals with Alzheimer's? They are bereft of their mnemonic being. Those who have ministered to such people realize how music that has been known for a lifetime can give them back their memory and humanity, if even for an instant.

There is no easy way to get at this cluster of issues, no legalistic guarantees that will fix the problem. But what is certain is this: acceding to it is no solution. Doing all throwaway music is no solution. We have to sing with our children what is worth singing, what they and we can grow into rather that out of, so that on our deathbeds we will remember what is worth remembering. We have to sing the story—the psalms and canticles, especially—and serve our churches well with music that is worth their time and effort. That does not necessitate one style, and it does not mean no throw-away music or avoiding new things. I do not mean to minimize the problems, the pastoral ones especially, that we have to face. I do mean to say that one of our priorities is to ask about what's worth doing, to realize that those who came before us have some wisdom to impart about that, to trust that God and not the novelty of our ego-centered brainstorms will sustain the church, and then to proceed boldly without fear.

2. As I have suggested, music is related not simply to the story, but to the time in which the story unfolds. This gives the musician a peculiar and remarkable responsibility. The church musician tells time for the people. In part that is true in the way I have just described singing the story. But in part it is true in direct relation to a service of worship, since music spins itself out in time just the same as worship does. Music accompanies processions, either of all the people or of some of the people for everyone else. This processional nature of the pilgrim people on the move takes place in time. Music articulates that time, as in music that accompanies processions. Beyond that, music articulates worship itself. That is, the church musician is the one who controls the pace and the shape and flow of a service more than anyone else. Points of beginning, middle, and ending in an entrance rite, for example, or at the reading of lessons followed by sermon and hymn, or in receiving holy communion almost invariably have musical components that accompany them. They include silence, which is music's backdrop, and completion. The sensitive church musician handles this responsibility with great care and a tremendous sense of concern for the people and how the liturgy flows for them.

+ + +

I'm not telling you anything you don't know. I'm just bringing to consciousness what you already know.

- Who cares most about the church year? You who are the musicians. Why? Because you know instinctively by your vocation and calling that you have to be responsible for more than one style, more than one mode of articulation, more than one dynamic level, more than one part of the plot. You know by your vocation that you can't have Easter without Lent, that there's no feast without a fast, no resurrection without the cross. You know by your vocation that you are responsible for the fullness of the story.

- Why do you who are musicians seek to learn from the best practitioners of your craft? Partly to learn about technique, literature, and many details, to be sure. But the finest practitioners of our craft teach us much more—something about how the story and time get articulated in our worship. We learn from them how a service takes shape. They teach us about key relationships, pacing, tempos, phrasing—not only in self-contained pieces, but in worship services where those pieces fit together in a coherent whole.

Again, I'm just bringing to consciousness for you what you already know. No matter how many times you find it denied by those who should know better, some clergy and lay leaders among them, I'm encouraging you to do what you know with compassionate boldness for your people.

1 *The [Episcopal] Hymnal 1982* (New York: The Church Hymnal Corporation, 1985), nos. 448 and 449.

2 Archbishop John of Chicago, et al., *Sacred Music: Its Nature and Function* (Chicago: The Department of Liturgical Music, Orthodox Church in America, 1977), p. 2.

Chapter 5

Church Music as Gift of God

Woe to those who sing idle songs to the sound of the harp,
and like David invent for themselves instruments of music.

Amos 6:5

This is a curious quotation to use when considering music as a gift. It seems to attack music generally, to undo the whole musical enterprise in the church, to silence us, and to cut out the roots of our musical heritage by undermining David who is the primal musical figure in the Bible.

We need to realize that Amos was probably singing this rebuke in prophetic fashion. The quotation is laid out like a poem, which for the ancient Israelites, even more than for us, was close to if not actually perceived to be music—much the way we talk of a hymn without distinguishing between the text and the music. If Amos were attacking music and literally meant to silence it, he chose a strange vehicle, music itself, to do the job.

If you look at the verse before and after this text, it becomes very clear what Amos is up to. He's not intent on silencing music. He's angry about its perversion and its use to console those who neglect justice. Here's the text in its context.

Alas, for those who lied on beds of ivory,
    and lounge on their couches,
and eat lambs from the flock,
    and calves from the stall;
who sing idle songs to the sound of the harp,
    and like David improvise on instruments of music;
who drink from bowls,
    and anoint themselves with the finest oils,
but are not grieved over the ruin of Joseph.

Amos 6:4–7

In the previous chapter, Amos had belted out the more famous passage: "Take away from me the noise of your songs…but let justice roll down…." (Amos 5:23–24). In place of doing justice and caring about selling Joseph and the people into slavery, says Amos, you lounge on your couches, sing idle songs, and invent (or improvise on) musical instruments.

Amos is the prophet, the gadfly, the bur under the saddle, the perennial reminder of how easy it is to turn God's gift of music into a perverse and evil nightmare that isolates us from humanity's needs, keeps us from singing to God, and then naturally deters us from the demands of justice.[1] We are not well-served by missing the point. The point is not to do away with music. The point is not to misuse it. The point is to concern ourselves with justice and to steward God's gift of music with integrity. How, then, is music a gift of God?

Music is a joy and delight with which God graces the creation. We do not bargain for it. We do not deserve it. It is simply freely given, there for the hearing, a joyous overflow of creation's goodness.

This gift can be viewed in many ways. One is the way Luther viewed it. Oskar Soehngen points out that Luther was forever amazed that music, this "unique gift of God's creation," comes from "the sphere of miraculous audible things," just like the Word of God.[2] This perceptive insight points to music as a gift and to the close relationship between music and words: both are audible, words amazingly can be sung, and it is all gift, in this case, as you might expect for Luther, close to proclamation.

Joseph Gelineau looks at the gift of music from another angle. He called music "God's daughter," given to humanity to signify the love of Christ. Viewed this way, music almost takes on the character of a sacramental sign that points beyond itself to pure love.[3] The Eastern Orthodox church often takes a similar view that music can "reflect the harmony of heaven" and "can provide us with a foretaste of the splendor of the Age to come."[4]

These views always bring with them music's power to uplift, transform, refresh, and recreate the heart and soul.[5] John Calvin asserts this when he calls music a "gift of God deputed" for "recreating" humanity and giving us pleasure.[6] While Ulrich Zwingli in the sixteenth century related the refreshment of music to secular play, thereby giving music no relevance at all to worship,[7] even liberal Protestantism today, which often begins with a similar presupposition, may nonetheless call music "revelatory." Robert Shaw, for instance, when he was installed as Minister of Music of the First Unitarian Church of Cleveland, Ohio, quoted J. W. N. Sullivan, and argued that "a work of art may indeed be a 'revelation.'"[8] Many Christians would disagree with what Shaw meant by revelation and worship, but his use of the term "revelation" shows how all worshiping traditions grapple with the gift of music and with its power.

When the gift of music is encountered, as we have just seen, the question of its power among us is immediately in play. If music is not perverted—and the perversions are all too pervasive and dispiriting—there are two ways music's power can be viewed.

The first is in what might be called its ritual function. Apart from articulating time—already a ritual function—the very presence of sound makes us present to one another at worship in a way our physical presence does not. That is, we have to disclose ourselves to one another when we sing. Kathleen Harmon, Music Director for the Institute for Liturgical Ministry in Dayton, Ohio, recently pointed this out when she said we can't choose to have no visual appearance, but we can choose to have no auditory one.[9] That is, our faces cannot be hidden unless we veil them, but our voices cannot be heard unless we sing. Our signature as face is always present to others, but our signature as voice is not present to others until we make sounds. We express ourselves and become vulnerable to God and to one another in our song in a unique way.

The second point is closely related to the first. It has to do with healing. Possibly because it is so powerful and deep, for most of the church most of the time little is said about this. Yet congregations and choirs who sing know penetrating health in a profound way, even if they seldom articulate it or may not even know how to articulate it. They know they not only disclose themselves to God and to one another, but they know a deep wholeness and shalom that comes in their singing.

One can approach this reality at several levels, first by simply pointing to its physicality. Breath, vocal folds, posture, body, and mind are called into play and united in a uniquely healing whole when one sings. When a whole body of people sings, a common breath, body, and mind are engaged in a larger healing whole. But that only begins to probe the healing. One must go on to say that the whole body is greater than the sum of its parts and the individual singer transported beyond what she or he could do alone. Beyond that, there is a picture of justice here, as Jonathon Edwards said, and beyond that something intangible, something about health and healing that congregations and choirs experience in their innermost beings.

Some people may call this sacramental. Like Luther, I would not. There is profound gift here, especially in connection with or around word and sacraments. Alexander Schmemann is certainly right when he says that the whole world is sacramental.[10] In that sense, music too can be called sacramental. Albert Blackwell cannot be too easily dismissed when he talks about music as "potentially sacramental," and Joseph Gelineau's sense of music as sacramental sign is not to be neglected either. I think, however, that to suggest that music is especially sacramental or uniquely akin to what the church has called sacraments is to mix categories and to drain words of their content. More seriously, it can all too easily turn "sacramental" from God's gift to our craft, since to be sacramental the gift of music requires crafting in a way the signs of water or bread and wine do not. The result is to regard sacraments as less than they are and music as less than it is.

Neither of these or any other of music's powerful characteristics that one might isolate is possible without music's gift as art. It is popular today to belittle art and music as art, probably because art has been misused as a classist vehicle of control and can all too easily smack of an unlovely and undesirable elitism. But we do not have to accede to classist pretensions that deny all sorts and conditions of the human race their artistic birthright. We do not have to treat people with such contempt. We do not have to embrace elitism to affirm music as art. To avoid music's artistic nature is to deny music itself.

The point here is not to draw a distinction between high and low art or high and folk art, as if music could be divided in such an artificial way. Music is music, some of it good and some of it less than good. Folk or high art has nothing to do with its quality. Nor is the point that music in worship is not functional. Of course it is functional, Gebrauchsmusik, to use the technical term. That does not preclude the finest art either. Nor is the point that a composer of church music ought to set out to make great art by staring at the art itself. That's a self-defeating enterprise, rather like putting a Stradivarius in an enclosure in a museum so one can stare at it but not hear it.

The point is that any music that bears repetition, music on which time and effort are worth being spent, will be fine art. The point is that music in worship, the highest activity of humankind, will of necessity invoke the finest craft and that, in turn, has the potential to issue in the finest art. Precisely because music serves a greater good than itself gives it the best chance to be the finest art. Gregorian chant, Palestrina motets, Bach cantatas, black spirituals, and innumerable hymns with their tunes are prime examples—amazing art and amazing gifts to the whole human race.

+ + +

How does the gift of music relate to the church musician's role? The cantor is the steward of God's gracious gift of music. Since this gift is so powerful, the steward receives a tremendous power as the deputy. The power can easily be misused not only by perverting it and isolating ourselves from the concerns for justice and health, but for selfish ends of ego gratification and personal control. The cantor is called, therefore, to the paradox of using the power that is granted in music, but using it with restraint on behalf of God in Christ from whom all blessings—including this one—flow.

That paradox brings with it another. The cantor knows that the preacher or lector can stumble over a word here or there, and still the message will have its impact. To stumble over a note is much more dangerous; the message's impact will dissipate much more quickly when there is a musical error, partly because there is more of art. So the cantor is constantly constrained to achieve an excellence and perfection that is ultimately never humanly possible. That drives the church musician to rehearse and practice every detail until it is right, for without practice there is the certainty that the necessary perfection and excellence will never be achieved. The paradox is that even with disciplined rehearsing there is no guarantee. The musician who is at all sensitive knows that when she or he finally gets it right, that too is a gift for which the only appropriate response is thanksgiving. (And even then it's never really "right." Each "right" only leads to a higher conception of what "getting it right" means.)

+ + +

Having determined what to do is not quite enough. Three further components of the cantor's role need to be isolated. They fit under the issue of how to approach the task.

First, the cantor is serving a specific people. As I indicated earlier, your responsibility as cantor is to allow the song of the people of God in your place to find expression. You do that not by superimposing an unattainable ideal and then flagellating yourself and your parish for never reaching it. Of course you challenge yourself and your people, but the ideal relates to the people and choir and musicians you have to work with because God is present among them with the song. Your responsibility is to allow the song among your people to find expression. That is the ideal.

This is not to suggest that there are no standards. There are standards for music just as the Ten Commandments are standards for living. The church as a community of grace, however, begins with grace, not with the law. So the cantor begins with God's gracious gift of music among a given people, not with arbitrary legal constructs and rules of constraint. The incipient song must find expression. Essentially, this means selecting durable music that is worth the people's time and effort, then doing things musically so that the people are invited to sing. The examples of a beautifully shaped phrase, organ playing that breathes with the people, rhythm that pulsates, and melodies that sing all will do more to give the song expression than heavy-handed rules and legalistic constraints. Any musical person knows this instinctively. So does your congregation.

Second, the cantor's craft must be exercised with kindness and compassion. Many musicians in our culture get by with being temperamental because we somehow believe that artists are naturally temperamental and should be humored. This is especially true of some secular instrumental and choral conductors who regularly throw temper tantrums and treat people poorly to achieve their ends.

Temperamental conductors have in the past, and to a certain extent still today, virtually become an accepted cultural reality for musicians and the general public, and church musicians have often felt compelled to imitate their example. The cantor knows another reality, that people are to be treated with respect because they are loved by God. Music is for people. People are not for music. Apart from the practical reality that if you want your people to sing you have to treat them well, the deeper truth is that nobody has the right to treat other human beings poorly.

This is not to suggest that cantors can be more perfect than those who work at any other profession. Like all musicians and all people, cantors will sometimes get angry, lose their tempers, and be temperamental. Because musicians hear a perfection that is not humanly possible, they are perhaps especially prone to anger when it is not forthcoming. Hearing and seeking perfection, however, is not the root of the problem. The problem is to discipline ourselves around a larger ideal. That ideal is kindness and compassion. We gather around the song God gives us, not around the personality of the conductor, no matter how good he or she may be.

Third, a word needs to be said specifically about leadership of the song. It is a complex matter that requires great sensitivity. There are times, such as Easter Sunday morning on an explosive hymn of resurrection joy, when the organ can appropriately drive the congregation with a powerful rhythmic punch. Generally, the organist or church musician should lead—sensitively, but lead. There are other times, however, such as the singing of some responsorial psalms or prayers, when neither organ nor conducting seems appropriate, as the community finds its own tempo with only a breath from the cantor to set things in motion. George Black is one of the past presidents of the Hymn Society in the United States and Canada and former professor of French and Church Music at Huron College, University of Western Ontario. I once heard him say that a community of love will sing together, that to tamper with the people's prayer is a tricky business, and that the cantor needs faithfully to take some risks, like sometimes letting the people set their own tempo. Those are profoundly true observations that cantors need to ponder in their hearts and experience with their communities of faith. Church musicians ought not always conduct or overtly control everything with the voice or organ or other instruments. That is not leadership. It is more an exhibition of our own problems, our own insecurities, and our unwillingness to allow the people's voice to find expression.

Leadership, then, involves a balance of many factors. The style of music (a rhythmic chorale from the sixteenth century has a different "ideal" tempo than a nineteenth century tune), the nature of the text, the place in the service, the time of year, the time of day, the weather, the size and acoustics of the building, the acoustical key of the building, the tradition of the congregation, the nature of the community (young or old, good or ill health), the size of the community, the pacing of the presider, and your own tendencies are among the things you need to consider. They require thoughtful attention before the service, but you also must respond in the moment to the event of music-making itself. Wonderful surprises can happen if you are sensitive and simply allow them to occur. Charismatic communities highlight this more than the rest of us, but the Holy Spirit graces all our worship and leads us all into ever-new truths.

The gift of music is a wonder. It's no small thing, and it's your duty and delight to allow it to take voice among your people. You know this instinctively. I simply bring it to your consciousness and encourage you in it.

---

1 For more about this, see Paul Westermeyer, *Let Justice Sing: Hymnody and Justice* (Collegeville: The Liturgical Press, 1998).

2 Oskar Soehngen, "Fundamental Considerations for a Theology of Music," *The Musical Heritage of the Church*, Vol. VI (St. Louis: Concordia Publishing House, 1962), p. 15.

3 Joseph Gelineau, *Voices and Instruments in Christian Worship* (Collegeville: The Liturgical Press, 1964), p. 27.

4 Archbishop John, p. 3.

5 Ibid., p. 2.

6 Charles Garside, Jr., "Calvin's Preface to the Psalter: A Re-Appraisal," *The Musical Quarterly*, XXXVII (October 1951): 570.

7 See Charles Garside, Jr., *Zwingli and the Arts* (New Haven and London: Yale University Press, 1966).

8 Robert Shaw, "Music and Worship in the Liberal Church" (Typescript, September 25, 1967), p. 8.

9 At the *Worship 2000 Jubilee* of the Evangelical Lutheran Church in America in Chicago at St. Clement's Roman Catholic Church, July 12, 2000.

10 Alexander Schmemann, *For the Life of the World: Sacraments and Orthodoxy* (St. Vladimir's Seminary Press, 1973), p. 74.